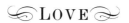

LOVE

PENHALIGON'S
SCENTED TREASURY
OF VERSE AND
PROSE

LOVE

EDITED BY SHEILA PICKLES

HARMONY BOOKS
NEW YORK

*This book is dedicated
to my love
D. R.*

CONTENTS

Introduction 6

✑ Introduction ✑

Dear Reader,

   It is said that one can count those people one truly loves on the fingers of one hand. I pity those poor souls! I have never accepted this theory and doubt whether I could include everyone if I counted all my fingers and my toes too. I am extremely fortunate in having felt very loved all through my life, so loving has always come easily to me. Selecting these passages has given me time to reflect on the different ways one loves during the course of a lifetime and relive my own experiences.

   In childhood one takes the love one receives for granted. Maternal love, I feel, is the purest form of love – we accept it in innocence and it was only on becoming a mother myself, whispering sweet nothings to my babies and singing the same nursery rhymes that had been sung to me, that I realized: as one is loved, so one loves. Then, in their turn, with childhood behind them, most lads and lasses dream of love. Such lasses are Tess and the milkmaids at Talbothay's Dairy, dreaming together of Angel Clare. Thackeray's words of caution to the young ladies might well have been those of my godmother Sheila, after whom I was named, whose love and cautioning endured long after I had gone down the aisle.

   The state of being in love is like none other, as David Copperfield finds out; it causes us to lose all sense of perspective, as Anna Karenina shows, and often brings grief to our families, like Shakespeare's heroines Juliet and Jessica. Unrequited love is the saddest state of all – for both those who have been rejected and those who have not yet dared to reach out their hands. Heathcliff was to turn almost bestial with jealousy and bitterness at

Cathy's marriage to Edgar Linton, and Mr. Rochester was driven to commit bigamy in order to marry Jane Eyre.

Let us feel compassion too for those who love outside the accepted boundaries of society, so well described by Lord Alfred Douglas.

It is quite possible to have very loving relationships which go on for years completely unacknowledged and, on reflection, these are some of the most rewarding. I am thinking in particular of the love of friends who share one's confidences, hopes and fears, beginning, perhaps, at school, just as Benjamin Disraeli describes, and continuing for a lifetime. My friends are precious to me and I am indebted to many of them, for their love has been tried and tested, and reciprocated unconditionally.

So love comes round full circle – the mother in her turn has to let her child go so that they may go on to love others. What greater test of love! One's heart goes out to Mr. Harding in *The Warden* who faces losing his daughter, and in *Silas Marner* Eppie is quick to reassure her adoring daddy that he is in fact gaining a son, rather than losing a daughter.

How lucky I am that love ran out to meet me with open arms and courted me with Romance. I have dedicated this book to that love who married me and with whom I share my life, in the optimism that in years to come we will agree that Old Love is Gold Love, Old Love is Best.

Sheila Pickles
Bath, 1988.

LOVE INSPIRED

"Love should run out to meet love
with open arms."

᳨᳨ Summer Night ᳨᳨

Now sleeps the crimson petal, now the white;
  Nor waves the cypress in the palace walk;
Nor winks the gold fin in the porphyry font:
The firefly wakens: waken thou with me.

  Now droops the milk-white peacock like a ghost,
And like a ghost she glimmers on to me.

  Now lies the Earth all Danaë to the stars,
And all thy heart lies open unto me.

  Now slides the silent meteor on, and leaves
A shining furrow, as thy thoughts in me.

  Now folds the lily all her sweetness up,
And slips into the bosom of the lake:
So fold thyself, my dearest, thou, and slip
Into my bosom and be lost in me.

LORD TENNYSON, 1809–1892

The Passionate Shepherd to His Love

COME live with me and be my Love,
And we will all the pleasures prove
That hills and valleys, dales and fields,
Or woods or steepy mountain yields.

And we will sit upon the rocks,
And see the shepherds feed their flocks
By shallow rivers, to whose falls
Melodious birds sing madrigals.

And I will make thee beds of roses
And a thousand fragrant posies;
A cap of flowers, and a kirtle
Embroider'd all with leaves of myrtle.

A gown made of the finest wool
Which from our pretty lambs we pull;
Fair-linèd slippers for the cold,
With buckles of the purest gold.

A belt of straw and ivy-buds
With coral clasps and amber studs:
And if these pleasures may thee move,
Come live with me and be my Love.

The shepherd swains shall dance and sing
For thy delight each May morning:
If these delights thy mind may move,
Then live with me and be my Love.

CHRISTOPHER MARLOWE. 1564-1593

Be Cautious

Be cautious then, young ladies; be wary how you engage. Be shy of loving frankly; never tell all you feel, or (a better way still) feel very little. See the consequences of being prematurely honest and confiding, and mistrust yourselves and everybody. Get yourselves married as they do in France, where the lawyers are the bridesmaids and confidants. At any rate, never have any feelings which may make you uncomfortable, or make any promises which you cannot at any required moment command and withdraw. That is the way to get on, and be respected, and have a virtuous character in Vanity Fair.

VANITY FAIR, WILLIAM MAKEPEACE THACKERAY, 1811–1863

～ Romeo and Juliet ～

But soft, what light through yonder window breaks?
It is the east, and Juliet is the sun.
Arise, fair sun, and kill the envious moon.
Who is already sick and pale with grief
That thou, her maid, art far more fair than she.
Be not her maid, since she is envious.
Her vestal livery is but sick and green,
And none but fools do wear it; cast it off.
   [*Enter Juliet aloft*]
It is my lady, O, it is my love.
O that she knew she were!
She speaks, yet she says nothing. What of that?
Her eye discourses; I will answer it.
I am too bold. 'Tis not to me she speaks.
Two of the fairest stars in all the heaven,
Having some business, do entreat her eyes
To twinkle in their spheres till they return.
What if her eyes were there, they in her head? –

The brightness of her cheek would shame those stars
As daylight doth a lamp; her eye in heaven
Would through the airy region stream so bright
That birds would sing and think it were not night.
See how she leans her cheek upon her hand.
O, that I were a glove upon that hand,
That I might touch that cheek!

Juliet Ay me.

Romeo [*aside*] She speaks.
O, speak again, bright angel; for thou art
As glorious to this night, being o'er my head,
As is a wingèd messenger of heaven
Unto the white upturnèd wond'ring eyes
Of mortals that fall back to gaze on him
When he bestrides the lazy-passing clouds
And sails upon the bosom of the air.

Juliet [*not knowing Romeo hears her*]
O Romeo, Romeo, wherefore art thou Romeo?
Deny thy father and refuse thy name,
Or if thou wilt not, be but sworn my love,
And I'll no longer be a Capulet.

Romeo [*aside*]
Shall I hear more, or shall I speak at this?

Juliet
'Tis but thy name that is my enemy.
Thou art thyself, though not a Montague.
What's Montague? It is nor hand, nor foot,
Nor arm, nor face, nor any other part
Belonging to a man. O, be some other name!
What's in a name? That which we call a rose
By any other word would smell as sweet.
So Romeo would, were he not Romeo called,
Retain that dear perfection which he owes
Without that title. Romeo, doff thy name,
And for thy name—which is no part of thee—
Take all myself.

WILLIAM SHAKESPEARE, 1564–1616

In a Gondola

THE moth's kiss, first!
 Kiss me as if you made me believe
You were not sure, this eve,
How my face, your flower, had pursed
Its petals up; so, here and there
You brush it, till I grow aware
Who wants me, and wide ope I burst.

The bee's kiss, now!
Kiss me as if you enter'd gay
My heart at some noonday,
A bud that dares not disallow
The claim, so all is render'd up,
And passively its shatter'd cup
Over your head to sleep I bow.

ROBERT BROWNING, 1812–1889

ೂ Queen Mab ೮ఀ

Mercutio
O, then I see Queen Mab hath been with you ...
She is the fairies' midwife, and she comes
In shape no bigger than an agate stone
On the forefinger of an alderman.
Her traces of the moonshine's watry beams
Her collars, of the smallest spider web;

Her whip, of cricket's bone, the lash of film;
Her wagoner, a small grey-coated gnat
Not half so big as a round little worm
Pricked from the lazy finger of a maid.
Her chariot is an empty hazelnut
Made by the joiner squirrel or old grub,
Time out o' mind the fairies' coachmakers.
And in this state she gallops night by night
Through lovers' brains, and then they dream of love;
O'er courtiers' knees, that dream on curtsies straight;
O'er ladies' lips, who straight on kisses dream,
Which oft the angry Mab with blisters plagues
Because their breaths with sweetmeats tainted are.
Sometime she gallops o'er a lawyers lip,
And then dreams he of smelling out a suit;
And sometime comes she with a tithe-pig's tail
Tickling a parson's nose as a lies asleep;
Then dreams he of another benefice.
Sometime she driveth o'er a soldier's neck,
And then dreams he of cutting foreign throats,
Of breaches, ambuscados, Spanish blades,
Of healths five fathom deep; and then anon
Drums in his ear, at which he starts and wakes,
And being thus frightened, swears a prayer or two,
And sleeps again. This is that very Mab
That plaits the manes of horses in the night,
And bakes the elf-locks in foul sluttish hairs,
Which once untangled much misfortune bodes.
This is the hag, when maids lie on their backs,
That presses them and learns them first to bear,
Making them women of good carriage.

ROMEO AND JULIET, WILLIAM SHAKESPEARE. 1564–1616

❦ Francesca and Paolo ❦

"Love, to which the gentle heart so quickly succumbs, possessed this man of my mortal beauty; and what came to pass wounds me eternally. Love, which frees no one loved from loving, so besotted me with him that, as you bear witness, it besotts me still. Love led us to one death: Caina awaits he who took life from us."

These were the words of these pitiful souls, and on hearing them, I bent my head so low and for so long that at last the Poet Virgil said to me: "What are you thinking?"

When I answered I began: "O woe, how many sweet thoughts, what great desire, brought them to this miserable end!"

Then I turned to them and began: "Francesca, your sorrows make me weep out of grief and pity. But tell me this: in the days of your sweet romance, how and when exactly did love make you sure of these uncertain desires?"

And she said to me: "There is nothing worse than to recall happiness in times of misery, as your mentor knows well. But if you really wish to know the very beginnings of our love, I shall tell you, although I can speak only through tears.

"We were reading one day of Lancelot in the clutches of love. We were alone and felt no shame. Often our eyes met across the page and we blushed; but it was in one sudden moment that we were won. When we read that the longed-for lips were kissed by such a lover, he, who would never then be parted from me, tremblingly kissed my lips. Galeotto was the name and author of the book. We read no more that day."

While the one spirit said all of this to me, the other wept so dolefully that I felt deathly weak with pity and fell down in a deathly faint.

INFERNO, DANTE ALIGHIERI, 1265–1321

Cleopatra

THE barge she sat in, like a burnish'd throne,
Burn'd on the water. The poop was beaten gold;
Purple the sails, and so perfumed that
The winds were love-sick with them; the oars were silver,
Which to the tune of flutes kept stroke, and made

The water which they beat to follow faster,
As amorous of their strokes. For her own person,
It beggar'd all description. She did lie
In her pavilion, cloth-of-gold, of tissue,
O'erpicturing that Venus where we see
The fancy out-work nature. On each side her
Stood pretty dimpled boys, like smiling Cupids,
With divers-colour'd fans, whose wind did seem
To glow the delicate cheeks which they did cool,
And what they undid did.

Agrippa O, rare for Antony!

Enobarbus Her gentlewomen, like the Nereides,
So many mermaids, tended her i' th' eyes,
And made their bends adornings. At the helm
A seeming mermaid steers. The silken tackle
Swell with the touches of those flower-soft hands
That yarely frame the office. From the barge
A strange invisible perfume hits the sense
Of the adjacent wharfs. The city cast
Her people out upon her; and Antony,
Enthron'd i' th' market-place, did sit alone,
Whistling to th' air; which, but for vacancy,
Had gone to gaze on Cleopatra too,
And made a gap in nature.

Agrippa Rare Egyptian!

Enobarbus Upon her landing, Antony sent to her,
Invited her to supper. She replied
It should be better he became her guest;
Which she entreated. Our courteous Antony,
Whom ne'er the word of 'No' woman heard speak,
Being barber'd ten times o'er, goes to the feast,
And for his ordinary pays his heart
For what his eyes eat only.

WILLIAM SHAKESPEARE, 1564–1616

—25—

᭡ᕽ The Declaration ᕽᳱ

As for the innumerable army of anæmic and tailorish persons who occupy the face of this planet with so much propriety, it is palpably absurd to imagine them in any such situation as a love-affair. A wet rag goes safely by the fire; and if a man is blind, he cannot expect to be much impressed by romantic scenery. Apart from all this many lovable people miss each other in the world, or meet under some unfavourable star. There is the nice and critical moment of declaration to be got over. From timidity or lack of opportunity a good half of possible love cases never get so far, and at least another quarter do there cease and determine. A very adroit person, to be sure, manages to prepare the way and out with his declaration in the nick of time. And then there is a fine solid sort of man, who goes on from snub to snub; and if he has to declare forty times, will continue imperturbably declaring, amid the astonished consideration of men and angels, until he has a favourable answer. I dare say, if one were a woman, one would like to marry a man who was capable of doing this, but not quite one who had done so. It is just a little bit abject, and somehow just a little bit gross; and marriages in which one of the parties has been thus battered into consent scarcely form agreeable subjects for meditation. Love should run out to meet love with open arms. Indeed, the ideal story is that of two people who go into love step for step, with a fluttered consciousness, like a pair of children venturing together into a dark room. From the first moment when they see each other, with a pang of curiosity, through stage after stage of growing pleasure and embarrassment, they can read the expression of their own trouble in each other's eyes. There is here no declaration properly so called; the feeling is so plainly shared, that as soon as the man knows what it is in his own heart, he is sure of what it is in the woman's.

VIRGINIBUS PUERISQUE, ROBERT LOUIS STEVENSON, 1850–1894

Algernon [*speaking very rapidly*]: Cecily, ever since I first looked upon your wonderful and incomparable beauty, I have dared to love you wildly, passionately, devotedly, hopelessly.

Cecily: I don't think that you should tell me that you love me wildly, passionately, devotedly, hopelessly. Hopelessly doesn't seem to make much sense, does it?

Algernon: Cecily! . . .

. . . I don't care for anybody in the whole world but you. I love you, Cecily. You will marry me, won't you?

Cecily: You silly boy! Of course. Why, we have been engaged for the last three months.

Algernon: For the last three months?

Cecily: Yes, it will be exactly three months on Thursday.

Algernon: But how did we become engaged?

Cecily: Well, ever since dear Uncle Jack first confessed to us that he had a younger brother who was very wicked and bad, you, of course, have formed the chief topic of conversation between myself and Miss Prism. And, of course, a man who is much talked about is always very attractive. One feels there must be something in him, after all. I dare say it was foolish of me, but I fell in love with you, Ernest.

Algernon: Darling. And when was the engagement actually settled?

Cecily: On the 14th of February last. Worn out by your entire ignorance of my existence, I determined to end the matter one way or the other, and after a long struggle with myself I accepted you under this dear old tree here. The next day I bought this little ring in your name, and this is the little bangle with the true lovers' knot I promised you always to wear.

Algernon: Did I give you this? It's very pretty, isn't it?

Cecily: Yes, you've wonderfully good taste, Ernest. It's the excuse I've always given for your leading such a bad life. And this is the box in which I keep all your dear letters. [*Kneels at table, opens box, and produces letters tied up with blue ribbon.*]

Algernon: My letters! But, my own sweet Cecily, I have never written you any letters.

Cecily: You need hardly remind me of that, Ernest. I remember only too well that I was forced to write your letters for you. I wrote always three times a week, and sometimes oftener.

Algernon: Oh, do let me read them, Cecily?

Cecily: Oh, I couldn't possibly. They would make you far too conceited. [*Replaces box.*] The three you wrote me after I had broken off the engagement are so beautiful, and so badly spelled, that even now I can hardly read them without crying a little.

Algernon: But was our engagement ever broken off?

Cecily: Of course it was. On the 22nd of last March. You can see the entry if you like. [*Shows diary.*] "To-day I broke off my engagement with Ernest. I feel it is better to do so. The weather still continues charming."

Algernon: But why on earth did you break it off? What had I done? I had done nothing at all. Cecily, I am very much hurt indeed to hear you broke it off. Particularly when the weather was so charming.

Cecily: It would hardly have been a really serious engagement if it hadn't been broken off at least once. But I forgave you before the week was out.

OSCAR WILDE, 1854–1900

❧ *Wanton Maidens* ❧

THE wanton Maidens him espying, stood
  Gazing a while at his vnwonted guise;
Then th'one her selfe low ducked in the flood,
Abasht, that her a straunger did avise:
But th'other rather higher did arise,
And her two lilly paps aloft displayd,
And all, that might his melting hart entise
To her delights, she vnto him bewrayd:
The rest hid vnderneath, him more desirous made.

FAERIE QUEEN. EDMUND SPENSER. 1552–1599

✒ Loving Angel ✒

TESS'S heart ached. There was no concealing from herself the fact that she loved Angel Clare, perhaps all the more passionately from knowing that the others had also lost their hearts to him. There is contagion in this sentiment, especially among women. And yet that same hungry heart of hers compassionated her friends. Tess's honest nature had fought against this, but too feebly, and the natural result had followed.

"I will never stand in your way, nor in the way of either of you!" she declared to Retty that night in the bedroom (her tears running down). "I can't help this, my dear! I don't think marrying is in his mind at all; but if he were even to ask me I should refuse him, as I should refuse any man."

"Oh! would you? Why?" said wondering Retty.

"It cannot be! But I will be plain. Putting myself quite on one side, I don't think he will choose either of you."

"I have never expected it—thought of it!" moaned Retty. "But O! I wish I was dead!"

The poor child, torn by a feeling which she hardly understood, turned to the other two girls who came upstairs just then.

"We be friends with her again," she said to them. "She thinks no more of his choosing her than we do."

So the reserve went off, and they were confiding and warm.

"I don't seem to care what I do now," said Marian, whose mood was tuned to its lowest bass. "I was going to marry a dairyman at Stickleford, who's asked me twice; but—my soul—I would put an end to myself rather'n be his wife now! Why don't ye speak, Izz?"

"To confess, then," murmured Izz, "I made sure to-day that he was going to kiss me as he held me; and I lay still

against his breast, hoping and hoping, and never moved at
all. But he did not. I don't like biding here at Talbothays
any longer! I shall go home."

The air of the sleeping-chamber seemed to palpitate
with the hopeless passion of the girls. They writhed
feverishly under the oppressiveness of an emotion thrust
on them by cruel Nature's law—an emotion which they
had neither expected nor desired. The incident of the day
had fanned the flame that was burning the inside of their
hearts out, and the torture was almost more than they
could endure. The differences which distinguished them
as individuals were abstracted by this passion, and each
was but portion of one organism called sex.

TESS OF THE D'URBERVILLES, THOMAS HARDY, 1840–1928

⚛ An American Custom ⚛

"I AM afraid your habits are those of a flirt," said Winterbourne, gravely.

"Of course they are," she cried, giving him her little smiling stare again. "I'm a fearful, frightful flirt! Did you ever hear of a nice girl that was not? But I suppose you will tell me now that I am not a nice girl."

"You're a very nice girl, but I wish you would flirt with me, and me only," said Winterbourne.

"Ah! thank you, thank you very much; you are the last man I should think of flirting with. As I have had the pleasure of informing you, you are too stiff."

"You say that too often," said Winterbourne.

Daisy gave a delighted laugh. "If I could have the sweet hope of making you angry, I would say it again."

"Don't do that; when I am angry I'm stiffer than ever. but if you won't flirt with me, do cease at least to flirt with your friend at the piano; they don't understand that sort of thing here."

"I thought they understood nothing else!" exclaimed Daisy.

"Not in young unmarried women."

"It seems to me much more proper in young unmarried women than in old married ones," Daisy declared.

"Well," said Winterbourne, "when you deal with natives you must go by the custom of the place. Flirting is a purely American custom; it doesn't exist here. So when you show yourself in public with Mr. Giovanelli, and without your mother— "

"Gracious! poor mother!" interposed Daisy.

"Though you may be flirting, Mr. Giovanelli is not; he means something else."

"He isn't preaching, at any rate," said Daisy, with vivacity. "And if you want very much to know, we are neither of us flirting; we are too good friends for that; we are very intimate friends."

"Ah!" rejoined Winterbourne, "if you are in love with each other it is another affair."

She had allowed him up to this point to talk so frankly that he had no expectation of shocking her by this ejaculation; but she immediately got up, blushing visibly, and leaving him to exclaim mentally that little American flirts were the queerest creatures in the world.

DAISY MILLER: A STUDY, HENRY JAMES, 1843–1916

❊ Be Married ❊

I FEEL sad when I don't see you. Be married, why won't you? And come to live with me. I will make you as happy as I can. You shall not be obliged to work hard; and when you are tired; you may lie in my lap and I will sing you to rest . . . I will play you a tune upon the violin as often as you ask and as well as I can; and leave off smoking, if you say so . . . I would always be very kind to you, I think, because I love you so well. I will not make you bring in wood and water, or feed the pig, or milk the cow, or go to the neighbors to borrow milk. Will you be married?

LETTER FROM AN AMERICAN SUITOR, 19th CENTURY

LOVE FULFILLED

"Because the birthday of my life
Is come, my love is come to me."

A Birthday

My heart is like a singing bird
  Whose nest is in a water'd shoot;
My heart is like an apple-tree
  Whose boughs are bent with thick-set fruit;
My heart is like a rainbow shell
  That paddles in halcyon sea;
My heart is gladder than all these,
  Because my love is come to me.

Raise me a daïs of silk and down;
  Hang it with vair and purple dyes;
Carve it in doves and pomegranates,
  And peacocks with a hundred eyes;
Work it in gold and silver grapes,
  In leaves and silver fleurs-de-lys;
Because the birthday of my life
  Is come, my love is come to me.

CHRISTINA GEORGINA ROSSETTI, 1830–1894

Lorenzo and Jessica

Lorenzo The moon shines bright. In such a night as this,
When the sweet wind did gently kiss the trees,
And they did make no noise–in such a night,
Troilus methinks mounted the Troyan walls,
And sigh'd his soul toward the Grecian tents,
Where Cressid lay that night.

Jessica In such a night
Did Thisby fearfully o'ertrip the dew,
And saw the lion's shadow ere himself,
And ran dismayed away.

Lorenzo In such a night
Stood Dido with a willow in her hand
Upon the wild sea-banks, and waft her love
To come again to Carthage.

Jessica In such a night
Medea gathered the enchanted herbs
That did renew old Æson.

Lorenzo In such a night
Did Jessica steal from the wealthy Jew,
And with an unthrift love did run from Venice
As far as Belmont.

Jessica In such a night
Did young Lorenzo swear he lov'd her well,
Stealing her soul with many vows of faith,
And ne'er a true one.

Lorenzo In such a night
Did pretty Jessica, like a little shrew,
Slander her love, and he forgave it her.

THE MERCHANT OF VENICE, WILLIAM SHAKESPEARE, 1564–1616

ANNA had been preparing herself for this meeting, had thought what she would say to him, but she did not succeed in saying any of it, overwhelmed by his passion. She tried to calm him, to calm herself, but it was too late. His emotion communicated itself to her. Her lips trembled so that for a long time she could not speak.

"Yes, you have taken possession of me, and I am yours," she got out at last, pressing his hands to her breast.

"So it had to be," he said. "As long as we live, so it must be. I know it now."

"That is true," she said, growing paler and paler and clasping his head. "Yet there is something terrible in this after all that has happened."

"It will pass, it will all pass; we shall be so happy! Our love, if it could grow stronger, would do so because of there being something terrible in it," he said, raising his head with a smile that showed his fine teeth.

She could not help responding with a smile—not to his words, but to the love in his eyes. She took his hand and stroked her cold cheeks and cropped hair with it.

"I hardly know you with this short hair. You have grown so pretty. A little boy! But how pale you are!"

"Yes, I am still very weak," she said, smiling. And her lips began trembling again.

"We'll go to Italy; you will soon get well," he said.

"Is it really possible that we could be like husband and wife, alone together, with our own family?" she said, looking close into his eyes.

"It only seems strange to me that it can ever have been otherwise."

"Stiva says *he* has agreed to everything, but I can't accept *his* generosity," she said, pensively gazing past Vronsky's face. "I don't want a divorce. It's all the same to me now. Only I don't know what he will decide about Seriozha."

He could not conceive how she could, at this moment of their reunion, remember and think of her son, of divorce. What did it all matter?

"Don't talk about that, don't think of it," he said, turning her hand over in his and trying to draw her attention to himself; but still she kept her eyes averted from him.

"Oh, why did I not die? It would have been better!" she said, and the tears streamed silently down her cheeks; but she tried to smile, so as not to grieve him.

Once Vronsky would have thought it disgraceful and impossible to decline the flattering offer of a post at Tashkent, which was a dangerous one, but now, without an instant's hesitation, he refused it and, observing disapproval in high quarters at this step, at once resigned his commission.

A month later Karenin was left alone in the house with his son, and Anna went abroad with Vronsky, not having obtained a divorce and having resolutely refused one.

ANNA KARENINA, COUNT TOLSTOY, 1828–1910

✒. The Song of Solomon ✒

I AM the rose of Sharon, *and* the lily of the valleys.

2 As the lily among thorns, so *is* my love among the daughters.

3 As the apple tree among the trees of the wood, so *is* my beloved among the sons. I sat down under his shadow with great delight, and his fruit *was* sweet to my taste.

4 He brought me to the banqueting house, and his banner over me *was* love.

OLD TESTAMENT

❧ *The Explanation* ❧

ELIZABETH'S spirits soon rising to playfulness again, she wanted Mr. Darcy to account for his having ever fallen in love with her. "How could you begin?" said she. "I can comprehend your going on charmingly, when you had once made a beginning; but what could set you off in the first place?"

"I cannot fix on the hour, or the spot, or the look, or the words, which laid the foundation. It is too long ago. I was in the middle before I knew that I *had* begun."

"My beauty you had early withstood, and as for my manners—my behaviour to *you* was at least always bordering on the uncivil, and I never spoke to you without rather wishing to give you pain than not. Now, be sincere; did you admire me for my impertinence?"

"For the liveliness of your mind, I did."

"You may as well call it impertinence at once. It was very little less. The fact is, that you were sick of civility, of deference, of officious attention. You were disgusted with the women who were always speaking and looking and thinking for *your* approbation alone. I roused and interested you, because I was so unlike *them*. Had you not been really amiable, you would have hated me for it; but, in spite of the pains you took to disguise yourself, your feelings were always noble and just; and, in your heart, you thoroughly despised the persons who so assiduously courted you. There—I have saved you the trouble of accounting for it; and really, all things considered, I begin to think it perfectly reasonable. To be sure, you know no actual good of me—but nobody thinks of *that* when they fall in love."

PRIDE AND PREJUDICE, JANE AUSTEN, 1775–1817

The Sun Rising

Busy old fool, unruly Sun,
  Why dost thou thus,
Through windows, and through curtains, call on us?
Must to thy motions lovers' seasons run?
  Saucy pedantic wretch, go chide
  Late school-boys and sour prentices,
  Go tell Court-huntsmen that the King will ride,
  Call country ants to harvest offices;
Love, all alike, no season knows nor clime,
Nor hours, days, months, which are the rags of time.

  Thy beams so reverend and strong
  Why shouldst thou think?
I could eclipse and cloud them with a wink,
But that I would not lose her sight so long.
  If her eyes have not blinded thine,
  Look, and to-morrow late tell me,
  Whether both th'Indias of spice and mine
  Be where thou left'st them, or lie here with me.
Ask for those kings whom thou saw'st yesterday.
And thou shalt hear, " All here in one bed lay. "

  She's all states, and all princes I;
  Nothing else is;
Princes do but play us; compar'd to this,
All honour's mimic, all wealth alchemy.
  Thou sun art half as happy as we,
  In that the world's contracted thus;
  Thine age asks ease, and since thy duties be
To warm the world, that's done in warming us.
Shine here to us, and thou art everywhere;
This bed thy centre is, these walls, thy sphere.

JOHN DONNE, 1572–1631

The Rose Did Caper

THE Rose did caper on her cheek—
Her Bodice rose and fell—
Her pretty speech—like drunken men—
Did stagger pitiful—

Her fingers fumbled at her work—
Her needle would not go—
What ailed so smart a little Maid—
It puzzled me to know—

Till opposite—I spied a cheek
That bore *another* Rose—
Just opposite—Another speech
That like the Drunkard goes—

A Vest that like her Bodice, danced—
To the immortal tune—
Till those two troubled—little Clocks
Ticked softly into one.

EMILY DICKINSON, 1830–1886

❧ *The Disciple* ❧

WHEN Narcissus died the pool of his pleasure changed
from a cup of sweet waters into a cup of salt tears,
and the Oreads came weeping through the woodland that
they might sing to the pool and give it comfort.

And when they saw that the pool had changed from a
cup of sweet waters into a cup of salt tears, they loosened
the green tresses of their hair and cried to the pool and
said, "We do not wonder that you should mourn in this
manner for Narcissus, so beautiful was he."

"But was Narcissus beautiful?" said the pool.

"Who should know that better than you?" answered
the Oreads. "Us did he ever pass by, but you he sought for,
and would lie on your banks and look down at you, and in
the mirror of your waters he would mirror his own
beauty."

And the pool answered, "But I loved Narcissus
because, as he lay on my banks and looked down at me, in
the mirror of his eyes I saw ever my own beauty mirrored.

OSCAR WILDE, 1854–1900

Love

ALL thoughts, all passions, all delights,
Whatever stirs this mortal frame,
All are but ministers of Love,
And feed his sacred flame.

Oft in my waking dreams do I
Live o'er again that happy hour,
When midway on the mount I lay,
Beside the ruin'd tower.

The moonshine, stealing o'er the scene,
Had blended with the lights of eve;
And she was there, my hope, my joy,
My own dear Genevieve!

She lean'd against the armèd man,
The statue of the armèd Knight;
She stood and listen'd to my lay,
Amid the lingering light . . . .

She half enclosed me with her arms,
She press'd me with a meek embrace;
And bending back her head, look'd up,
And gazed upon my face.

'Twas partly love, and partly fear,
And partly 'twas a bashful art,
That I might rather feel, than see,
The swelling of her heart.

I calm'd her fears, and she was calm,
And told her love with virgin pride;
And so I won my Genevieve,
My bright and beauteous Bride.

LOVE, SAMUEL TAYLOR COLERIDGE, 1772–1834

Blissful

ALL this time, I had gone on loving Dora, harder than ever. Her idea was my refuge in disappointment and distress, and made some amends to me, even for the loss of my friend. The more I pitied myself, or pitied others, the more I sought for consolation in the image of Dora. The greater the accumulation of deceit and trouble in the world, the brighter and the purer shone the star of Dora high above the world. I don't think I had any definite idea where Dora came from, or in what degree she was related to a higher order of being but I am quite sure I should have scouted the notion of her being simply human, like any other young lady, with indignation and contempt.

If I may so express it, I was steeped in Dora. I was not merely over head and ears in love with her, but I was saturated through and through. Enough love might have been wrung out of me, metaphorically speaking, to drown anybody in; and yet there would have remained enough within me, and all over me, to pervade my entire existence.

DAVID COPPERFIELD, CHARLES DICKENS, 1812–1870

Holiday Gown

In holiday gown, and my new-fangled hat,
  Last Monday I tripped to the fair;
I held up my head, and I'll tell you for what,
  Brisk Roger I guessed would be there:
He woos me to marry whenever we meet,
  There's honey sure dwells on his tongue!
He hugs me so close, and he kisses so sweet,
  I'd wed—if I were not too young.

Fond Sue, I'll assure you, laid hold on the boy,
  (The vixen would fain be his bride)
Some token she claimed, either ribbon or toy,
  And swore that she'd not be denied:
A top-knot he bought her, and garters of green,
  Pert Susan was cruelly stung;
I hate her so much, that, to kill her with spleen,
  I'd wed—if I were not too young.

He whispered such soft pretty things in mine ear!
  He flattered, he promised, and swore!
Such trinkets he gave me, such laces and gear,
  That, trust me,—my pockets ran o'er:
Some ballads he bought me, the best he could find,
  And sweetly their burthen he sung;
Good faith! he's so handsome, so witty, and kind,
  I'd wed—if I were not too young.

The sun was just setting, 'twas time to retire,
  (Our cottage was distant a mile)
I rose to be gone—Roger bowed like a squire,
  And handed me over the stile:
His arms he threw round me—love laughed in his eye,
  He led me the meadows among,
There pressed me so close, I agreed, with a sigh,
  To wed—for I was not too young.

JOHN CUNNINGHAM, 1729-1773

Laura and Lizzie Asleep

Golden head by golden head,
  Like two pigeons in one nest
Folded in each other's wings,
They lay down in their curtained bed:
Like two blossoms on one stem,
Like two flakes of new-fall'n snow,
Like two wands of ivory
Tipped with gold for awful kings.
Moon and stars gazed in at them,
Wind sang to them lullaby
Lumbering owls forbore to fly,
Not a bat flapped to and fro
Round their nest:
Cheek to cheek and breast to breast
Locked together in one nest.

CHRISTINA GEORGINA ROSSETTI, 1830–1894

LOVE UNREQUITED

"All's over, then: does truth sound bitter
As one at first believes?"

We'll Go No More A-Roving

So, we'll go no more a-roving
   So late into the night,
Though the heart be still as loving,
   And the moon be still as bright.

For the sword outwears its sheath,
   And the soul wears out the breast,
And the heart must pause to breathe,
   And love itself have rest.

Though the night was made for loving,
   And the day returns too soon,
Yet we'll go no more a-roving
   By the light of the moon.

LORD BYRON, 1788–1824

The Lost Mistress

ALL'S over, then: does truth sound bitter
    As one at first believes?
Hark, 'tis the sparrows' good-night twitter
    About your cottage eaves!

And the leaf-buds on the vine are woolly,
    I noticed that, to-day;
One day more bursts them open fully
    — You know the red turns gray.

To-morrow we meet the same then, dearest?
    May I take your hand in mine?
Mere friends are we,—well, friends the merest
    Keep much that I resign:

For each glance of the eye so bright and black.
    Though I keep with heart's endeavour,—
Your voice, when you wish the snowdrops back,
    Though it stay in my soul for ever!—

Yet I will but say what mere friends say,
    Or only a thought stronger;
I will hold your hand but as long as all may,
    Or so very little longer!

ROBERT BROWNING, 1872–1889

✑ Meg in Love ✑

Meg meanwhile had apparently forgotten the matter, and was absorbed in preparations for her father's return; but all of a sudden a change seemed to come over her, and, for a day or two, she was quite unlike herself. She started when spoken to, blushed when looked at, was very quiet, and sat over her sewing, with a timid, troubled look on her face. To her mother's inquiries she answered that she was quite well, and Jo's she silenced by begging to be let alone.

"She feels it in the air—love, I mean—and she's going very fast. She's got most of the symptoms,—is twittery and cross, doesn't eat, lies awake, and mopes in corners. I caught her singing that song he gave her, and once she said 'John,' as you do, and then turned as red as a poppy. Whatever shall we do?" said Jo, looking ready for any measures, however violent.

"Nothing but wait. Let her alone, be kind and patient, and father's coming will settle everything," replied her mother.

Little Women, Louisa May Alcott, 1832–1888

❧ Cathy and Heathcliff ❧

You teach me how cruel you've been—cruel and
false. Why did you despise me? Why did you
betray your own heart, Cathy? I have not one word
of comfort. You deserve this. You have killed
yourself. Yes, you may kiss me, and cry, and wring
out my kisses and tears; they'll blight you—they'll
damn you. You loved me; then what right had you to
leave me? What right—answer me—for the poor
fancy you felt for Linton? Because misery, and
degradation, and death, and nothing that God or
Satan could inflict would have parted us, you, of
your own free will, did it. I have not broken your
heart—you have broken it; and in breaking it you
have broken mine. So much the worse for me that I
am strong. Do I want to live? What kind of living
will it be, when you—O God—would you like to live
with your soul in the grave?

WUTHERING HEIGHTS, EMILY BRONTË, 1818–1848

Modern Love

A ND what is love? It is a doll dress'd up
For idleness to cosset, nurse, and dandle;
A thing of soft misnomers, so divine
That silly youth doth think to make itself
Divine by loving, and so goes on
Yawning and doting a whole summer long,
Till Miss's comb is made a pearl tiara,
And common Wellingtons turn Romeo boots;
Then Cleopatra lives at number seven,
And Antony resides in Brunswick Square.
Fools! if some passions high have warm'd the world,
If Queens and Soldiers have play'd deep for hearts,
It is no reason why such agonies
Should be more common than the growth of weeds.
Fools! make me whole again that weighty pearl
The Queen of Egypt melted, and I'll say
That ye may love in spite of beaver hats.

JOHN KEATS, 1795–1821

Annabel Lee

IT was many and many a year ago,
  In a kingdom by the sea,
That a maiden there lived whom you may know
  By the name of Annabel Lee;—
And this maiden she lived with no other thought
  Than to love and be loved by me.

She was a child and *I* was a child,
  In this kingdom by the sea,
But we loved with a love that was more than love—
  I and my Annabel Lee—
With a love that the wingéd seraphs of Heaven
  Coveted her and me.

And this was the reason that, long ago,
  In this kingdom by the sea,
A wind blew out of a cloud by night
  Chilling my Annabel Lee;
So that her highborn kinsmen came
  And bore her away from me,
To shut her up in a sepulchre
  In this kingdom by the sea.

The angels, not half so happy in Heaven,
  Went envying her and me:—
Yes! that was the reason (as all men know,
  In this kingdom by the sea)
That the wind came out of a cloud, chilling
  And killing my Annabel Lee.

But our love it was stronger by far than the love
  Of those who were older than we—
  Of many far wiser than we—

And neither the angels in Heaven above
　　Nor the demons down under the sea,
Can ever dissever my soul from the soul
　　Of the beautiful Annabel Lee:–

For the moon never beams without bringing me dreams
　　Of the beautiful Annabel Lee;
And the stars never rise but I see the bright eyes
　　Of the beautiful Annabel Lee;
And so, all the night-tide, I lie down by the side
Of my darling, my darling, my life and my bride,
　　In her sepulchre there by the sea–
　　In her tomb by the side of the sea.

EDGAR ALLEN POE, 1809–1849

Perfect Woman

SHE was a phantom of delight
When first she gleam'd upon my sight;
A lovely apparition, sent
To be a moment's ornament;
Her eyes as stars of twilight fair;
Like twilight's, too, her dusky hair;
But all things else about her drawn
From May-time and the cheerful dawn;
A dancing shape, an image gay,
To haunt, to startle, and waylay.

I saw her upon nearer view,
A Spirit, yet a Woman too!
Her household motions light and free,
And steps of virgin liberty;
A countenance in which did meet
Sweet records, promises as sweet;
A creature not too bright or good
For human nature's daily food;
For transient sorrows, simple wiles,
Praise, blame, love, kisses, tears, and smiles.

And now I see with eye serene
The very pulse of the machine;
A being breathing thoughtful breath,
A traveller between life and death;
The reason firm, the temperate will,
Endurance, foresight, strength, and skill;
A perfect Woman, nobly plann'd,
To warn, to comfort, and command;
And yet a Spirit still, and bright
With something of angelic light.

WILLIAM WORDSWORTH. 1770-1850

A Solemn Passion

AFTER a youth and manhood passed half in unutterable misery and half in dreary solitude, I have for the first time found what I can truly love—I have found *you*. You are my sympathy—my better self—my good angel—I am bound to you with a strong attachment. I think you good, gifted, lovely: a fervent, a solemn passion is conceived in my heart; it leans to you, draws you to my centre and spring of life, wraps my existence about you—and, kindling in pure, powerful flame, fuses you and me in one.

It was because I felt and knew this, that I resolved to marry you. To tell me that I had already a wife is empty mockery: you know now that I had but a hideous demon. I was wrong to attempt to deceive you; but I feared a stubbornness that exists in your character. I feared early instilled prejudice: I wanted to have you safe before hazarding confidences. This was cowardly: I should have appealed to your nobleness and magnanimity at first, as I do now—opened to you plainly my life of agony—described to you my hunger and thirst after a higher and worthier existence—shown to you, not my *resolution* (that word is weak), but my resistless *bent* to love faithfully and well, where I am faithfully and well loved in return. Then I should have asked you to accept my pledge of fidelity, and to give me yours: Jane—give it me now.

JANE EYRE, CHARLOTTE BRONTË, 1816–1855

Love in the Valley

UNDER yonder beech-tree single on the green-sward,
  Couch'd with her arms behind her golden head,
Knees and tresses folded to slip and ripple idly,
  Lies my young love sleeping in the shade.
Had I the heart to slide an arm beneath her,
  Press her parting lips as her waist I gather slow,
Waking in amazement she could not but embrace me:
  Then would she hold me and never let me go?

Shy as the squirrel and wayward as the swallow,
  Swift as the swallow along the river's light
Circleting the surface to meet his mirror'd winglets,
  Fleeter she seems in her stay than in her flight.
Shy as the squirrel that leaps among the pine-tops,
  Wayward as the swallow overhead at set of sun,
She whom I love is hard to catch and conquer,
  Hard, but O the glory of the winning were she won!

When her mother tends her before the laughing mirror,
  Tying up her laces, looping up her hair,
Often she thinks, were this wild thing wedded,
  More love should I have, and much less care.
When her mother tends her before the lighted mirror,
  Loosening her laces, combing down her curls,
Often she thinks, were this wild thing wedded,
  I should miss but one for many boys and girls.

Heartless she is as the shadow in the meadows
  Flying to the hills on a blue and breezy noon.
No, she is athirst and drinking up her wonder:
  Earth to her is young as the slip of the new moon.
Deals she an unkindness, 'tis but her rapid measure,
  Even as in a dance: and her smile can heal no less:
Like the swinging May-cloud that pelts the flowers
      with hailstones,
  Off a sunny border, she was made to bruise and bless . . .

GEORGE MEREDITH, 1828-1909

✥ To His Coy Mistress ✥

H AD we but world enough, and time,
This coyness lady were no crime.
We would sit down, and think which way
To walk, and pass our long loves day.
Thou by the Indian Ganges side
Should'st rubies find: I by the tide
Of Humber would complain. I would
Love you ten years before the flood:
And you should if you please refuse
Till the conversion of the Jews.

My vegetable love should grow
Vaster than empires, and more slow.
An hundred years should go to praise
Thine eyes, and on thy forehead gaze.
Two hundred to adore each breast:
But thirty thousand to the rest.
An age at least to every part,
And the last age should show your heart.
For lady you deserve this state:
Nor would I love at lower rate.
But at my back I alwaies hear
Time's winged charriot hurrying near;
And yonder all before us lye
Deserts of vast eternity.
Thy beauty shall no more be found;
Nor, in thy marble vault, shall sound
My echoing song: then worms shall try
That long preserv'd virginity:
And your quaint honour turn to dust;
And into ashes all my lust.
The grave's a fine and private place,
But none I think do there embrace.
Now therefore, while the youthful hew
Sits on they skin like morning dew
And while thy willing soul transpires
At every pore with instant fires,
Now let us sport us while we may;
And now, like am'rous birds of prey,
Rather at once our time devour,
Than languish in his slow-chapt pow'r
Let us roll all our strength, and all
Our sweetness, up into one ball:
And tear our pleasures with rough strife,
Thorough the iron gates of life.
Thus, though we cannot make our sun
Stand still, yet we will make him run.

ANDREW MARVELL. 1621–1678

❧ *Two Loves* ❧

"WHAT is thy name?" he said, "My name is Love."
Then straight the first did turn himself to me
And cried, "He lieth, for his name is Shame,
But I am Love, and I was wont to be
Alone in this fair garden, till he came
Unasked by night; I am true Love, I fill
The hearts of boy and girl with mutual flame."
Then sighing said the other, "Have thy will,
I am the Love that dare not speak its name."

TWO LOVES, LORD ALFRED DOUGLAS, 1870–1945

LOVE EVERLASTING

"I love thee to the depth and breadth and height
My soul can reach"

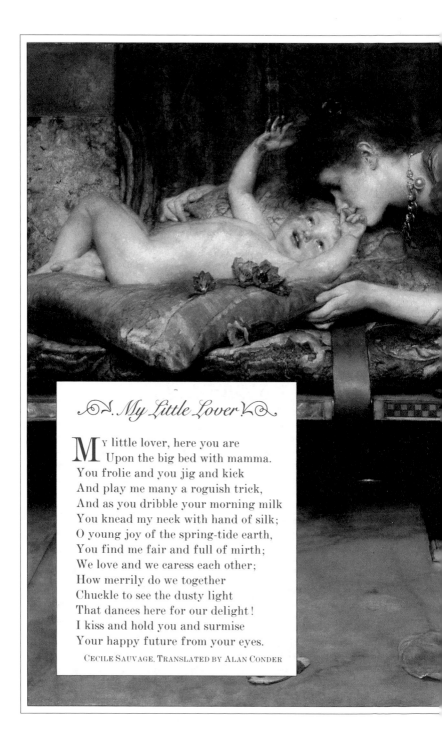

᧞ My Little Lover ᧞

M Y little lover, here you are
  Upon the big bed with mamma.
You frolic and you jig and kick
And play me many a roguish trick,
And as you dribble your morning milk
You knead my neck with hand of silk;
O young joy of the spring-tide earth,
You find me fair and full of mirth;
We love and we caress each other;
How merrily do we together
Chuckle to see the dusty light
That dances here for our delight!
I kiss and hold you and surmise
Your happy future from your eyes.

CECILE SAUVAGE, TRANSLATED BY ALAN CONDER

❧ Schoolboy Friendship ❧

At school, friendship is a passion. It entrances the being; it tears the soul. All loves of afterlife can never bring its rapture, or its wretchedness; no bliss so absorbing, no pangs of jealousy or despair so crushing and so keen! What tenderness and what devotion; what illimitable confidence, infinite revelations of inmost thoughts; what ecstatic present and romantic future; what bitter estrangements and what melting reconciliations; what scenes of wild recrimination, agitating explanations, passionate correspondence; what insane sensitiveness, and what frantic sensibility; what earthquakes of the heart and whirlwinds of the soul are confined in that simple phrase, a schoolboy's friendship!

CONINGSBY, BENJAMIN DISRAELI, 1804–1881

❋❋ Hiawatha's Childhood ❋❋

B y the shores of Gitche Gumee
   By the shining Big-Sea-Water,
Stood the wigwam of Nokomis,
Daughter of the Moon, Nokomis.
Dark behind it rose the forest,
Rose the black and gloomy pine-trees,
Rose the firs with cones upon them;
Bright before it beat the water,
Beat the clear and sunny water,
Beat the shining Big-Sea-Water.

There the wrinkled, old Nokomis
Nursed the little Hiawatha,
Rocked him in his linden cradle,
Bedded soft in moss and rushes,
Safely bound with reindeer sinews;
Stilled his fretful wail by saying,
" Hush ! the Naked Bear will hear thee !"
Lulled him into slumber, singing,
" Ewa-yea ! my little owlet !
Who is this, that lights the wigwam
With his great eyes lights the wigwam ?
Ewa-yea ! my little owlet !"

THE SONG OF HIAWATHA.
HENRY WADSWORTH LONGFELLOW. 1807–1882

Amelia's Boy

In this room was all Amelia's heart and treasure. Here it was that she tended her boy, and watched him through the many ills of childhood, with a constant passion of love. The elder George returned in him somehow, only improved, as if come back from heaven. In a hundred little tones, looks, and movements, the child was so like his father, that the widow's heart thrilled as she held him to it; and he would often ask the cause of her tears. It was because of his likeness to his father, she did not scruple to tell him. She talked constantly to him about this dead father, and spoke of her love for George to the innocent and wondering child; much more than she ever had done to George himself, or to any confidante of her youth. To her parents she never talked about this matter; shrinking from baring her heart to them. Little George very likely could understand no better than they; but into his ears she poured her sentimental secrets unreservedly, and into his only. The very joy of this woman was a sort of grief, or so tender, at least, that its expression was tears. Her sensibilities were so weak and tremulous, that perhaps they ought not to be talked about in a book.

Vanity Fair. William Makepeace Thackeray. 1811–1863

❧ A Father's Concern ❧

MR. HARDING was not the man to judge harshly of any one, much less of the daughter whom he now loved better than any living creature; but still he did judge her wrongly at this moment. He knew that she loved John Bold; he fully sympathised in her affection; day after day he thought more of the matter, and, with the tender care of a loving father, tried to arrange in his own mind how matters might be so managed that his daughter's heart should not be made the sacrifice to the dispute which was likely to exist between him and Bold. Now, when she spoke to him for the first time on the subject, it was natural that he should think more of her than of himself, and that he should imagine that her own cares, and not his, were troubling her.

He stood silent before her awhile, as she gazed up into his face, and then kissing her forehead he placed her on the sofa.

"Tell me, Nelly," he said (he only called her Nelly in his kindest, softest, sweetest moods, and yet all his moods were kind and sweet), "tell me, Nelly, do you like Mr. Bold – much?"

She was quite taken aback by the question. I will not say that she had forgotten herself, and her own love in thinking about John Bold, and while conversing with Mary: she certainly had not done so. She had been sick at heart to think, that a man of whom she could not but own to herself that she loved him, of whose regard she had been so proud, that such a man should turn against her father to ruin him. She had felt her vanity hurt, that his affection for her had not kept him from such a course; had he really cared for her, he would not have risked her love by such an outrage; but her main fear had been for her father, and when she spoke of danger, it was of danger to him and not to herself.

THE WARDEN, ANTHONY TROLLOPE, 1815–1882

❧ A Mother's Joy ❧

How the floodgates were opened, and mother and daughter wept, when they were together embracing each other in this sanctuary, may readily be imagined by every reader who possesses the least sentimental turn. When don't ladies weep? At what occasion of joy, sorrow, or other business of life? and, after such an event as a marriage, mother and daughter were surely at liberty to give way to a sensibility which is as tender as it is refreshing. About a question of marriage I have seen women who hate each other kiss and cry together quite fondly. How much more do they feel when they love! Good mothers are married over again at their daughters' weddings: and as for subsequent events, who does not know how ultra-maternal grandmothers are?—in fact a woman, until she is a grandmother, does not often really know what to be a mother is. Let us respect Amelia and her mamma whispering and whimpering and laughing and crying in the parlour and the twilight. Old Mr. Sedley did. *He* had not divined who was in the carriage when it drove up. He had not flown out to meet his daughter, though he kissed her very warmly when she entered the room (where he was occupied, as usual, with his papers and tapes and statements of accounts), and after sitting with the mother and daughter for a short time, he very wisely left the little apartment in their possession.

VANITY FAIR. WILLIAM MAKEPEACE THACKERAY. 1811–1863

❦ Gaining a Son ❧

HAPPILY the sunshine fell more warmly than usual on the lilac tufts the morning that Eppie was married, for her dress was a very light one. She had often thought, though with a feeling of renunciation, that the perfection of a wedding dress would be a white cotton, with the tiniest pink sprig at wide intervals; so that when Mrs. Godfrey Cass begged to provide one, and asked Eppie to choose what it should be, previous meditation had enabled her to give a decided answer at once.

Seen at a little distance as she walked across the churchyard and down the village, she seemed to be attired in pure white, and her hair looked like the dash of gold on a lily. One hand was on her husband's arm, and with the other she clasped the hand of her father Silas.

"You won't be giving me away, father," she had said before they went to church; "you'll only be taking Aaron to be a son to you."

SILAS MARNER, GEORGE ELIOT (MARY ANNE CROSS), 1819–1880

☙ Sonnet ☙

L ET me not to the marriage of true minds
   Admit impediments. Love is not love
Which alters when it alteration finds,
Or bends with the remover to remove:
O, no! it is an ever-fixed mark.
That looks on tempests and is never shaken;
It is the star to every wand'ring bark,
Whose worth's unknown, although his height be taken.
Love's not Time's fool, though rosy lips and cheeks
Within his bending sickle's compass come;
Love alters not with his brief hours and weeks,
But bears it out even to the edge of doom:—
    If this be error and upon me proved,
    I never writ, nor no man ever loved.

WILLIAM SHAKESPEARE, 1564–1616

How Do I Love Thee?

PORTUGUESE SONNET

How do I love thee: Let me count the ways.
I love thee to the depth and breadth and height
My soul can reach, when feeling out of sight
For the ends of Being and ideal Grace.
I love thee to the level of every day's
Most quiet need, by sun and candlelight.
I love thee freely, as men strive for Right;
I love thee purely, as they turn from Praise.
I love thee with the passion put to use
In my old griefs, and with my childhood's faith.
I love thee with a love I seemed to lose
With my lost saints,—I love thee with the breath,
Smiles, tears, of all my life!—and, if God choose,
I shall but love thee better after death.

ELIZABETH BARRETT BROWNING, 1806-1861

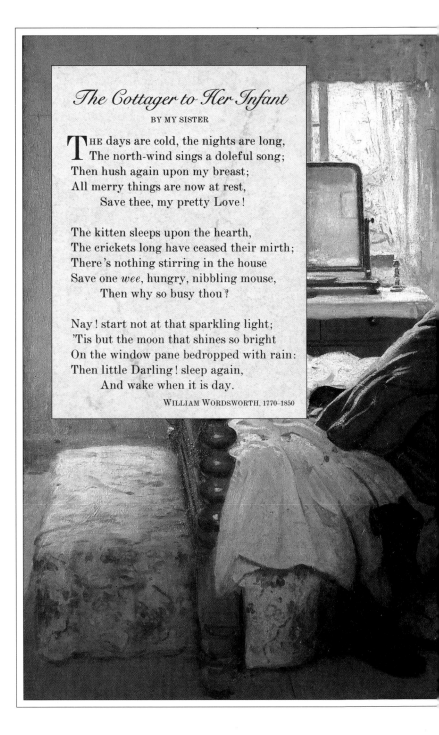

The Cottager to Her Infant

BY MY SISTER

THE days are cold, the nights are long,
  The north-wind sings a doleful song;
Then hush again upon my breast;
All merry things are now at rest,
    Save thee, my pretty Love!

The kitten sleeps upon the hearth,
The crickets long have ceased their mirth;
There's nothing stirring in the house
Save one *wee*, hungry, nibbling mouse,
    Then why so busy thou?

Nay! start not at that sparkling light;
'Tis but the moon that shines so bright
On the window pane bedropped with rain:
Then little Darling! sleep again,
    And wake when it is day.

WILLIAM WORDSWORTH, 1770–1850

When She Comes Home

WHEN she comes home again! A thousand ways
    I fashion, to myself, the tenderness
Of my glad welcome: I shall tremble—yes;
And touch her, as when first in the old days
I touched her girlish hand, nor dared upraise
Mine eyes, such was my faint heart's sweet distress.
Then silence: And the perfume of her dress:
The room will sway a little, and a haze
Cloy eyesight—soul-sight, even—for a space:
And tears—yes; and the ache here in the throat,
To know that I so ill-deserve the place
Her arms make for me; and the sobbing note
I stay with kisses, ere the tearful face
Again is hidden in the old embrace.

JAMES WHITCOMB RILEY. 1849–1916

ᦒ·Of Love and Champagne·ᦒ

Tʜᴇʏ sat down to table, and the waiter having handed the wine card to Forestier, Madame de Marelle exclaimed: "Give these gentlemen whatever they like, but for us iced champagne, the best, sweet champagne."

The Ostend oysters were brought in, tiny and plump, like little ears enclosed in shells, and melting between the tongue and the palate like salted bon-bons. Then, after the soup, a trout was served, as rose-tinted as a young girl, and the guests began to talk.

They spoke at first of a current scandal and then they began to talk of love. Without admitting it to be eternal, Duroy understood it as enduring, creating a bond, a tender friendship, a confidence. The union of the senses was only a seal to the union of hearts. But he was angry at

the outrageous jealousies, melodramatic scenes and un-
pleasantnesses which almost always accompany ruptures.

When he ceased speaking, Madame de Marelle replied:
" Yes, it is the only good thing in life, and we often spoil it
by preposterous unreasonableness. "

Madame Forestier, who was toying with her knife,
added: " Yes–yes–it is pleasant to be loved. "

And she seemed to be carrying her dream farther, to be
thinking things that she dared not give words to.

As the first entrée was slow in coming, they sipped
from time to time a mouthful of champagne and nibbled
bits of crust. And the thought of love slowly intoxicated
their souls, as the bright wine, rolling drop by drop down
their throats, fired their blood and perturbed their minds.

The waiter brought in some lamb cutlets, delicate and
tender, upon a thick layer of asparagus tips.

" Ah! this is good, " exclaimed Forestier; and they ate
slowly, enjoying the delicate meal and the vegetables as
smooth as cream.

Duroy resumed: " For my part, when I love a woman,
everything in the world disappears. " He said this in a
tone of conviction.

Madame Forestier murmured in accents of indiffer-
ence: " There is no happiness comparable to that of the
first hand-clasp, when the one asks: ' Do you love me ? ' and
the other replies, ' Yes '. "

BEL AMI. GUY DE MAUPASSANT. 1850–1893

✄ *Slippers and Rice* ✄

S AME old slippers,
  Same old rice,
Same old glimpse of
Paradise.

WILLIAM JAMES LAMPTON,
1859–1917

⟶❧ When You Are Old ❧⟵

WHEN you are old and gray and full of sleep,
  And nodding by the fire, take down this book,
And slowly read, and dream of the soft look
Your eyes had once, and of their shadows deep;

How many loved your moments of glad grace,
And loved your beauty with love false or true,
But one man loved the pilgrim soul in you,
And loved the sorrows of your changing face;

And bending down beside the glowing bars,
Murmur, a little sadly, how Love fled
And paced upon the mountains overhead
And hid his face amid a crowd of stars.

W B YEATS. 1865–1939

❧ For A Golden Wedding ❧

D AWN love is silver,
   Wait for the west:
Old love is gold love—
   Old love is best.

KATHARINE LEE BATES, 1859–1929